art
in a
cup

CUPS AND SAUCERS
1860-1950

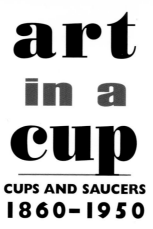

Pomegranate

SAN FRANCISCO

Pomegranate Communications, Inc.
Box 6099, Rohnert Park, CA 94927
800-227-1428
www.pomegranate.com

Pomegranate Europe Ltd.
Fullbridge House, Fullbridge
Maldon, Essex CM9 4LE
England

ISBN 0-7649-1622-X
Pomegranate Catalog No. AA108

Pomegranate publishes books of
postcards on a wide range of subjects.
Please contact the publisher for more information.

Cover designed by Patrice Morris
Printed in Korea
10 09 08 07 06 05 04 03 02 01   10 9 8 7 6 5 4 3 2 1

To facilitate detachment of the postcards from this book, fold each card along its perforation line before tearing.

Cups and saucers, like all dishware, are created for practical use. But practical use does not preclude artistic expression. The cups and saucers featured here are more than utilitarian objects; they are exquisite expressions of the movements and styles popular during the time of their manufacture, which include Japonaiserie, Arts and Crafts, Art Deco, and postwar influences. This delicate tableware, manufactured between 1860 and 1950, blurs the distinction between fine art and decorative design. Henry van de Velde, Louis Comfort Tiffany, Josef Hoffmann, Gertrude and Otto Natzler, Jean Luce and many others designed these porcelain, glass, earthenware, or silver vessels for such well-known companies as Meissen, Royal Doulton, and the Paul Revere Pottery.

These cups and saucers have graced turn-of-the-century New York City drawing rooms and the meeting places of Russia's avant-garde. Each is a unique piece of art with stunning details: the delicate arabesque of the silver teacup and saucer created by Tiffany, the geometric design of Hoffmann's black striped porcelain mocha cup, and the refreshing polka dots of Suzanne Lalique's teacup and saucer garnished with a hand-painted bow. The Historical Design gallery in New York City first featured these objects in a 1996 exhibition titled *Art in a Cup,* which showcased over one hundred cups and saucers. The most visually delightful have been chosen for this book of thirty postcards.

art in a cup
CUPS AND SAUCERS 1860–1950

Renaissance Revival teacup and saucer, 1860
Sterling silver with applied leaf, vine and bird motifs
Tiffany & Co., New York

BOX 6099 ROHNERT PARK CA 94927

Pomegranate

art in a cup
CUPS AND SAUCERS 1860–1950

Gothic Revival chocolate cup and saucer, c. 1860
Gilt double-bodied porcelain cup with reticulated outer surface
Imperial & Royal Porcelain Manufactory, Vienna

BOX 6099 ROHNERT PARK CA 94927

Pomegranate

ART IN A CUP

art in a cup
CUPS AND SAUCERS 1860–1950

Japanesque teacup and saucer, 1874
Soft paste porcelain hand-painted with floral motifs
George Jones & Sons Ltd., Stoke on Trent, Staffordshire

BOX 6099 ROHNERT PARK CA 94927

Pomegranate

art in a cup
CUPS AND SAUCERS 1860–1950

Lotus lapover-edge cup with saucer, 1879
Sterling silver and copper, silver applications
Tiffany & Co., New York

BOX 6099   ROHNERT PARK   CA 94927

Pomegranate

art in a cup
CUPS AND SAUCERS 1860–1950

Waterlily cup with butterfly handle and lily pad saucer, c. 1880
Hand-painted and gilded porcelain
Moore Bros., Staffordshire

BOX 6099   ROHNERT PARK   CA 94927

Pomegranate

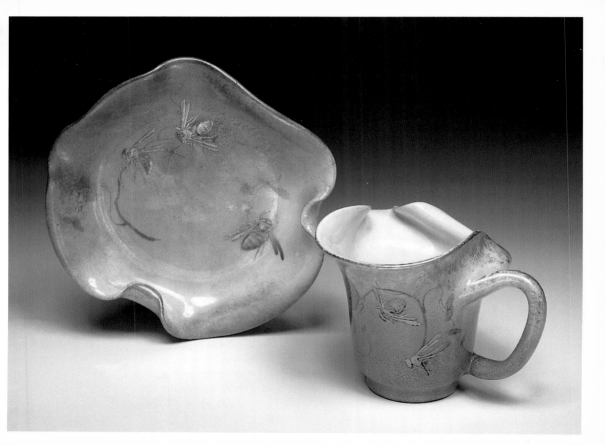

art in a cup
CUPS AND SAUCERS 1860–1950

Clément Massier, France
Bees distorted-form teacup and saucer, c. 1890
Earthenware with hand-painted and gilt decoration
Faiences d'Art, Golfe-Juan

BOX 6099   ROHNERT PARK   CA 94927

Pomegranate

art in a cup
CUPS AND SAUCERS 1860–1950

Alf Wallander, Sweden
Mocha cup and saucer from the *Iris* service, 1897
Hand-painted porcelain with applied decoration
Rörstrand Porcelain Factory, Lidköping

Pomegranate

BOX 6099   ROHNERT PARK   CA 94927

96

Maxim's
3 Rue Royale

RESTAURANT GRILL-ROOM

The GLACIER   Téléphone 244-92

coy   2

Pommery   40
de Sie Russe   x   2

Sole Polignac
Côtes d'agne

Faure
M

voiture   70 f
5
162

VEUVE POMMERY

art in a cup
CUPS AND SAUCERS 1860–1950

Maxim's de Paris, France
Champagne Cork demitasse cup and saucer, c. 1900
Transfer- and hand-painted porcelain
Porcelaine de Paris

BOX 6099   ROHNERT PARK   CA 94927

Pomegranate

art in a cup
CUPS AND SAUCERS 1860–1950

Maurice Dufrène, France
Teacup and saucer with abstract floral design, c. 1902
Hand-painted porcelain
Designed for La Maison Moderne, Paris (made in Limoges)

BOX 6099 ROHNERT PARK CA 94927

Pomegranate

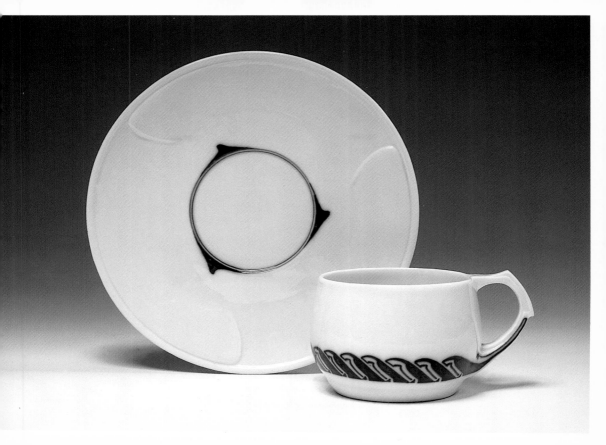

art in a cup
CUPS AND SAUCERS 1860–1950

Henry van de Velde, Belgium (active in Germany)
Peitschenhieb teacup and saucer, 1903–04
Porcelain decorated in underglaze blue
Königlich Sächsische Porzellan-Manufaktur, Meissen, Saxony

BOX 6099   ROHNERT PARK   CA 94927

Pomegranate

art in a cup
CUPS AND SAUCERS 1860–1950

J. W. van Rossum, The Netherlands
Waterlily cup and saucer, 1904
Eggshell porcelain with hand-painted decoration
Rozenburg, Haagsche Plateelbakkerij, Den Haag

Pomegranate

BOX 6099   ROHNERT PARK   CA 94927

art in a cup
CUPS AND SAUCERS 1860-1950

Alphonse Sandoz, France
Buttress cup and saucer, 1904
Porcelain with underglaze decoration
Manufacture Nationale de Sèvres

Pomegranate

BOX 6099   ROHNERT PARK   CA 94927

art in a cup
CUPS AND SAUCERS 1860-1950

George Logan, Glasgow
Glasgow Rose teacup and saucer, c. 1905
Porcelain with stencil-painted decoration
Foley Pottery, Staffordshire (Peacock Pottery)

Pomegranate

BOX 6099   ROHNERT PARK   CA 94927

art in a cup
CUPS AND SAUCERS 1860-1950

Josef Hoffmann, Austria
Black-and-white mocha cup and saucer, c. 1910
Hand-painted porcelain for Josef Bock, Vienna
Pfeiffer & Löwenstein, Schlackenwerth, Bohemia

BOX 6099   ROHNERT PARK   CA 94927

Pomegranate

art in a cup
CUPS AND SAUCERS 1860–1950

Oriental Poppy teacup and saucer, 1912
Faience with transfer decoration
Royal Doulton, Lambeth & Burslem, Staffordshire

BOX 6099 ROHNERT PARK CA 94927

Pomegranate

art in a cup
CUPS AND SAUCERS 1860-1950

The Saturday Evening Girls, USA
Tree and Landscape teacup and saucer, 1913
Hand-painted earthenware
Paul Revere Pottery, Boston, Massachusetts

BOX 6099   ROHNERT PARK   CA 94927

Pomegranate

art in a cup
CUPS AND SAUCERS 1860–1950

Nikolai Suetin, Russia
Suprematist teacup and saucer, 1923
Hand-painted porcelain
State Porcelain Factory, Petrograd

BOX 6099 ROHNERT PARK CA 94927

Pomegranate

art in a cup
CUPS AND SAUCERS 1860–1950

Hendrik Petrus Berlage, The Netherlands
Modernist teacup and saucer, 1924
Molded glass
Executed by Leerdam Glassworks

BOX 6099   ROHNERT PARK   CA 94927

Pomegranate

art in a cup
CUPS AND SAUCERS 1860–1950

Walter Mutze
Abstract-design demitasse cup and saucer, 1927
Porcelain with painted decoration
Rosenthal Porzellan AG, Selb, Bavaria

Pomegranate

BOX 6099   ROHNERT PARK   CA 94927

art in a cup
CUPS AND SAUCERS 1860–1950

Hilde Adler (attributed), Austria
Art Deco demitasse cup and saucer, c. 1928
Hand-painted enamel on copper, brass handle
Schule Josef Hoffmann, Vienna

BOX 6099   ROHNERT PARK   CA 94927

Pomegranate

art in a cup
CUPS AND SAUCERS 1860-1950

Lili Schultz (attributed), Germany
Coffee cup and saucer with concentric ring design, c. 1928
Nickeled copper with colored enamels, ebony handle
Enameling: Kunstgewerbeschule Burg Giebichenstein, Halle

ART IN A CVP

BOX 6099 ROHNERT PARK CA 94927

Pomegranate

art in a cup
CUPS AND SAUCERS 1860–1950

Suzanne Lalique, France
Polka Dots and Bow teacup and saucer, c. 1928
Hand-painted porcelain
Executed by Theodore Haviland, Limoges

BOX 6099   ROHNERT PARK   CA 94927

Pomegranate

art in a cup
CUPS AND SAUCERS 1860–1950

Jean Luce, France
Art Moderne coffee cup and saucer, c. 1929
Porcelain with gilding
Made in Paris at Luce's factory

BOX 6099   ROHNERT PARK   CA 94927

Pomegranate

art in a cup
CUPS AND SAUCERS 1860–1950

Josef Hoffmann, Austria
Abstract-design teacup on feet with saucer, 1929
Hand-painted porcelain
Wiener Porzellanfabrik Augarten, Vienna

BOX 6099 ROHNERT PARK CA 94927

Pomegranate

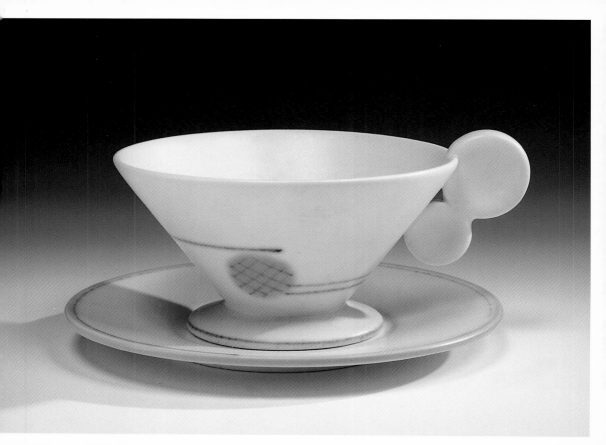

art in a **cup**
CUPS AND SAUCERS 1860–1950

Margarete Heymann-Marks, Germany
Disk-handled teacup and saucer, 1930
Faience with hand-painted decoration
Haël Werkstätten, Marwitz

BOX 6099   ROHNERT PARK   CA 94927

Pomegranate

art in a cup
CUPS AND SAUCERS 1860–1950

Crown Devon, Great Britain
Orient demitasse cup and saucer, 1930
Porcelain decorated in color enamels and gilding
S. Fielding & Co., Stoke on Trent, Staffordshire

Pomegranate

BOX 6099   ROHNERT PARK   CA 94927

art in a cup
CUPS AND SAUCERS 1860–1950

Vanessa Bell, Great Britain
Teacup and saucer with abstract leaf motif, c. 1932
Hand-painted earthenware
Made in Charleston, Sussex

Pomegranate

BOX 6099 ROHNERT PARK CA 94927

art in a cup
CUPS AND SAUCERS 1860-1950

Dorothy C. Thorpe, USA
Ball-handled teacup and saucer, c. 1940
Matte-finish porcelain in light pink and blue glaze
Porcelaine de Paris, France

Pomegranate

BOX 6099   ROHNERT PARK   CA 94927

art in a cup
CUPS AND SAUCERS 1860–1950

Gertrude and Otto Natzler, Austria (active in USA)
Black and chartreuse demitasse cups with tab handles and saucers, c. 1940
Manganese-glazed earthenware
Executed by the Natzlers, Los Angeles

BOX 6099   ROHNERT PARK   CA 94927

Pomegranate

art in a cup
CUPS AND SAUCERS 1860-1950

Heintz Schaubach, Germany
Mimosa Leaf teacup and saucer, c. 1950
Porcelain with black, white and gilt decoration
VEB Porcelain Factory, Unterweissbach

BOX 6099   ROHNERT PARK   CA 94927

Pomegranate